PERSONAL SPACE

PERSONAL SPACE: TRIP HAENISCH

RIZZOLI NEW YORK

New York · Paris · London · Milan

FOREWORD

by Courteney Cox

I have been interested / obsessed with architecture and design ever since I was a little kid and shared a room with my sister. I was constantly rearranging our twin beds and pillows—always looking for a fresh take!

Since then, I have been lucky enough to live in homes designed by such amazing California architects as John Lautner and A. Quincy Jones. Living in those unique places taught me how important and challenging it is to find the harmony between the design and architecture.

That's why I was so fortunate to meet Trip. He is someone who is extremely passionate about and understands all aspects of architecture. He taught me how important it is to get the interior "box" perfect before you worry about the furniture and lighting. I'd never thought like that before.

My Malibu house was the perfect place to learn the value of this.

There are several structures on the property, kind of like a compound. It's a place where I could have family and friends stay over, creating a community-like feeling that is hard to find in Los Angeles.

Michael Kovac, the architect, and Trip worked together seamlessly to make this dream come true.

Not only did I end up with my dream house, I had the best time in the process. I'm very particular and I have strong opinions. I'm not the type of person who would be content to just look on while the designer did all the work. Trip gave me that space. He is a great collaborator. Trip has such natural talent that it makes you feel at ease. He was able to create my vision while also pushing me beyond my comfort zone. Trip found the rare balance between comfort and beauty. He also became a great friend.

INTRODUCTION

by Susanna Salk

"I've always been an observer," says Trip Haenisch. "And I've always been interested in how spaces make me feel and in turn, I've learned how to create spaces to make other people feel at home. I like to go beyond just making a room feel pretty."

Emotion is a layer Haenisch knows can only come after the more pragmatic part of the interior equation is properly set: the necessity of good architecture. "I learned early on that you can't disguise bad interior architecture with beautiful furniture," says Haenisch. Having worked after college for IBM analyzing the efficiency levels of corporations, Haenisch more than understands the practical power of logistics and applied that skill when his career path turned to designing. "If you haven't created proper proportions, flow, and function then a house can't be efficient when it comes to living within it."

Yet it was perhaps the unpredictable nature of design that showed Haenisch the true spirit of what it means to live a well-lived life—those spontaneous elements that can't be charted or quantified, the impractical pleasures that helped him understand how rooms should make you feel. This invaluable education was given thanks to his mentor and former life partner, the designer extraordinaire Waldo Fernandez.

"I didn't have any kind of formal design training when I first came to Los Angeles years ago," says Haenisch, who drove out of his childhood driveway in Kansas City with nothing but his clothes and a television set strapped into the passenger seat of his Mazda and headed straight for Los Angeles. He knew only one friend there and slept on his apartment floor. But after meeting Fernandez, Haenisch soon found his footing and along the way, a point of view. "Traveling the world with Waldo, we were lucky enough to stay in some of its most iconic homes," remembers Haenisch. "Experiencing design as a houseguest was the best training I could have possibly had even though I didn't know yet that design was the path I was going to choose as a career."

A visit with the actress Elizabeth Taylor (who would become godmother to Fernandez and Haenisch's son, Jake) to the legendary fashion designer Gianni Versace's home on Lake Como was particularly indelible. "It was designed by Renzo Mongiardino and filled with amazing antiquities, artwork, inlaid floors, and velvets with tassels," recalls Haenisch. "It was so beautiful, I was afraid to sit down. But then Gianni came in, in a swimsuit and bare feet followed by his sister Donatella's young children running through in wet swimsuits. Suddenly I realized that the owner can give you permission, in their own way, to enjoy the space, and that a home's true mission was to simply be enjoyed."

Calvin Klein's Hamptons retreat on Georgica Pond, with its sweeping views to the Atlantic Ocean, was equally impressionable on Haenisch: "Calvin had ebonized the floors as dark as can be and the walls were crisp white with white drapery floating in the warm cross breeze. I then understood how something so restrained could still elicit such an emotional, visceral response."

Equally informative was the home Haenisch shared with Fernandez in Beverly Hills. "At one end of the living room was an enormous Roman head with a provenance dating back before the time of Christ and opposite that was an eighteenth-century gilded Italian console," remembers Haenisch. "Set on top was a slatted Crate & Barrel container planted with a white orchid, and hanging above that was a Jean-Michel Basquiat painting. It's the contrast of the unexpected that gives the ultimate beauty to a room."

Another lesson in his design schooling was collaborating in the Waldo Collection, a trade-only shop he shared with Fernandez in the 1980s filled with vintage furniture and accessories found on their trips from Morocco to Maine. "I'd love to watch how the masters, like Michael Taylor and Kalef Alaton, would shop the store and then see the pieces in situ personally or captured in the pages of *Architectural Digest*. From that I gleaned a lot," says Haenisch.

Haenisch's career has brought him a multitude of magazine covers, a celebrity clientele, and a place on the AD100 list as well as being named one of the *Hollywood Reporter*'s twenty most influential Los Angeles–based interior designers. "My goal is to articulate my clients' varied lifestyles, whether they're in Park City, Perugia, or Park Avenue, through personalized designs," says Haenisch.

Actress Courteney Cox's Malibu retreat was a tired 1950s affair but features spectacular Pacific views and precious privacy. Using vertical siding, bronzed-steel trim, and a plethora of white walls, Haenisch created a modern, barn-like compound that manages to feel completely appropriate in its beachfront setting. "The intent was to make it feel like a great old house that was contemporized," says Haenisch, who layered in a Hans Wegner ox chair covered in a lush mohair teddy bear fabric, colorful artwork from the likes of Massimo Vitali, and a comfortable-yet-sexy L-shaped sectional Haenisch designed himself. "Trip is such a talented designer," Cox says. "I love working with him because of his great taste and his ability to adapt to my style while maintaining his own."

With an equally savvy and sure hand, he reinterpreted actor Hank Azaria's 1932 Monterey Colonial in Bel Air by combining leathers, metals, and ceramics as well as linen, velvet, and wool with vintage pieces, such as French army lockers in the dressing room and a round steel worktable in the breakfast nook. He even roughed-up the too-smooth ebonized floor using wire brushes for it to feel highly personalized. "I've become more fearless because I've learned that when it comes to designing, there is no right or wrong answer," says Haenisch.

A mid-century house in the Trousdale section of Beverly Hills built in the late '60s for the famed *Brady Bunch* television producer Sherwood Schwartz was recently revamped for a client by keeping the lines of the house but updating the interiors. "I loved much of the original architecture but wanted to take it into the twenty-first century and the way people live today," says Haenisch. He replaced the floors with wide plank oak and switched out the sliding doors for a system that opened an entire wall of the house to the outside. "We did that in the master bedroom and the living room and it totally changed the feel of the house," says Haenisch, who also removed the wall that separated the kitchen from the family room, increasing the entertaining footprint. A cheeky yet apt nod to the property's past, Haenisch hung a photograph of Sherwood with the whole *Brady Bunch* family standing on that famous staircase and placed it on one of the walls in the house.

Future projects for Haenisch's West Hollywood–based firm include creating two homes from the ground up, which particularly excites Haenisch because, "I love being able to focus on the interior architecture," which is a good thing, as one of the plans encompasses over 27,000 square feet in Bel Air. The other home is by far smaller, yet by no means less of a creative challenge: "It's going to be a modern tree house in Hollywood, nestled in overgrown vegetation."

No matter the place or plan, the constant for Haenisch is never to be too attached once its evolution is underway. "There are myriad ways to make a house look beautiful and be of visual interest. I'll lay out a room, and ask the client, 'What do you think of this or that?' If the client isn't enthusiastic, I know now to just immediately move on. More than anything I want to know from my clients what they need." He ultimately delivers rooms that feel highly collected instead of decorated, layered with his trademark sense of warm sophistication that always welcomes, never intimidates, and often surprises—with a cohesive mix of art and furnishings, whether sourced via online auctions in Europe, flea markets, or vintage shops, including one of his favorites, Retro Inferno in Kansas City.

And if the existence of a piece that would help solve the puzzle does not exist, Haenisch is delighted to design it himself. "I recently created a custom dining table for art-loving clients in the Pacific Palisades," says Haenisch. "For the top, I was inspired by photographs of the earth from space by planetary spacecraft." In his head, the sky is the limit. "I love creating something that's personal only to my clients," he says. "That's so important in making the room ultimately feel like it's really theirs."

He also grasps the importance of keeping a sense of humor, so that even when things feel just right, there's still a sense of edge to keep the beautiful balance on its toes: "It's all about finding the fun and the contentment," says Haenisch.

Whether transforming a Memphis Group–style Tawaraya boxing ring into a bed for his son or putting a urinal in a cigar-and-poker room in a private home in California or fashioning an outdoor bed from cement outside his office window and covering it in boxwood and ivy, Haenisch keeps striving for the spontaneous style of his design heroes. "In my own house, I make sure to embrace things that make me laugh," says Haenisch. "I've put this big lifeguard chair I found while in Europe in my small pool area. The absurdity of it makes me smile every time I see it. Or the big gnarly tree trunk I found at an antique shop, which the dealer was going to slice up for tabletops. It was just so pretty I knew I had to have it for myself." It now sits in his backyard, with a huge lampshade on top. "I think you should have fun in your own home. I even love for my art to make me laugh." Case in point: one of his favorites from his extensive photography collection (he started collecting in the 1980s, inspired by friends and master photographers Herb Ritts and Bruce Weber) is the Terry Richardson photograph of Batman kissing Robin.

Constantly on the go, Haenisch sees little distinction between work and play, especially since so many of his clients have become friends. When home, you can usually find him swimming laps, pursuing a daily yoga practice, or reclining poolside with his son and friends watching Monday night football on an outdoor screen that projects from his bedroom. "I am a Midwesterner, a practical guy, and I'd hate to see my clients spend a bunch of money and then have rooms they just walk through. A home is not a museum but a manifestation of the owner's personality, the most intimate and personal of spaces they can occupy. If a room goes unused, then I feel as if I have not done my job."

PACIFIC
PALISADES

Trip Haenisch's clients, a couple with young children, purchased this property for its beautiful setting on a flat, large plot of land and its wonderfully proportioned rooms and appropriate scale. The newly constructed traditional-style home was built on "spec," which meant that it was done and in good condition, however it was also very generic with lots of white and lacking personality. So, the couple sought out Haenisch and encouraged him to think outside the box, as they envisioned something fun, a space that felt young and appropriate for them. Haenisch's mandate quickly became that of taking the "spec" out of the home while providing his clients with something interesting and engaging, elegant yet playful.

Haenisch understood that incorporating a bit of the unexpected would go a long way toward these goals, so he set out to infuse the spaces with unique combinations of color, surface, texture, and styles. In many of the rooms he employed dynamic wallpapers, which created visual interest while highlighting the architectural moldings. In each room he included something different: he used orange paint on the ceiling and orange and brown Claremont wallpaper in the library. Here, the moldings and paneling were painted in a rich, deep brown to underscore the room's cozy feel while grounding and softening the boldly used orange. In the dining room he installed Fromental wallpaper above the wainscoting and designed a custom dining table, the top of which is a mosaic that he created and had manufactured in Italy, and then he attached a base that he designed and had made locally. A map of the world inspired the complex pattern of the mosaic. For an intimately scaled powder room, Haenisch found a fabric that he paperbacked to use in the toilet room at the back of the powder room and then he designed wallpaper for the sink area to correspond with and compliment the fabric. The end result is both whimsical and dynamic, and playful sconces underscore this intention.

The kitchen was originally completely white so Haenisch saw it as an opportunity to add more color and painted it a shade of blue-gray. When it came to dealing with the bar, which functions as a transitional space between the kitchen and family room, he incorporated an indigo color that is also used on some of the upholstery in the adjacent family space.

Haenisch was interested in establishing a color narrative that would change as one moves into and through the home. The tone in the living room and dining rooms, both at the front of the house, is subtler, and as you move closer to the back of the house, toward the more private parts of the home, like the kitchen and family room, the tone intensifies. As a nod to this color transition, Haenisch designed a custom runner for the center hall that hosts an abstract design reminiscent of a lightning bolt running the length of the long runner. The hues in the runner transition from browns to gray, and then to indigo as it directs visitors from the front to the back of the house.

While many of the furnishings were custom and of Haenisch's own design, such as the coffee table in the family room, the dining table, most of the upholstery, and many of the carpets, Haenisch was also happy to infuse the spaces with some important period pieces, some of which he customized: a Vladimir Kagan sofa shares space in the living room with a traditional table and a set of Platner chairs. Here, Haenisch lacquered the table gray and powder-coated the Platner chairs in white and added antique leather on their seats.

Lighting also became an opportunity to provide some unexpected whimsy. While many of the lighting fixtures are vintage, some of them were commissioned for the space. Jason Koharik designed the pieces in the living room and also in the family room, for example, and Jeff Zimmerman designed the piece in the stairwell.

Haenisch is happy with how the creative foundation of this project has given his clients license to freely collect interesting pieces from different periods and styles and finish and personalize the home over time. He is also pleased with how the space is used and acknowledges that making a pretty house isn't difficult, but creating a home that gets used is more of a challenge. His clients use all of the rooms in the house, which Haenisch considers a major victory. He admits to knowing that his clients love living in the home and as they do, their additions only improve their space. The house, he had hoped, would foster and encourage that kind of collaborative involvement.

Page 11: The custom silk and wool runner gradates from gray—the predominate color in the living room on the left—and then to blue, the dominating hue in the family room at the end of the hallway. **Previous spread:** A late nineteenth-century oak trestle table hosts a Ryan Mennealy ceramic table lamp. An Annie Lapin painting hangs above. **Opposite:** Living room. Haenisch painted the vintage Scandinavian game table to blend with the wallpaper by David Bonk. The space also features a silkscreened Chuck Close self-portrait, a custom wool rug, a pair of plaster sconces by Richard Etts, and a custom nautilus-inspired chandelier from Collected by Jason Koharik. **Following spread:** Living room. A Robert Perry lounge chair sits across from the Vladimir Kagan sofa. A Friedrich Kunath work hangs above the Illum Wikkelso lounge chair.

Opposite: Dining room. Paper-backed silk covers the walls. The *Tournesol* mirror from Downtown is flanked by a pair of circa 1950 Swedish brass wall lamps. Three Dorothy Thorpe Lucite candle holders stand beneath a vintage 1950s light fixture. **Above:** The mosaic on the Haenisch-designed dining table was fabricated in Italy by Fantini Mosaici and is surrounded by Milo Baughman dining chairs.

Above: Powder room. Haenisch designed the striped wallpaper to coordinate with the paper-backed Designers Guild fabric in the toilet room. The pair of *Alouette* wall lamps are from Atelier Areti. **Opposite:** Library. The walls are clad in a French 1920s reproduction print from Adelphi Paper Hangings, while a custom pendant light from Collected by Jason Koharik illuminates the space, which also spotlights a Harbinger Gould cocktail table, a vintage tufted leather ottoman circa 1880, and a custom Roman shade by Haenisch. **Following spread, from left to right:** An Ellsworth Kelly work hangs above a pair of mid-century *Bella* chairs upholstered in Belgian linen; a custom wool rug from Fedora Design, a pair of Cappellini *Ribbon* stools, and a custom rolled arm sofa with printed linen throw pillows comingle.

Above: Breakfast nook. The custom banquette is covered in dove gray Naugahyde, while the Haenisch designed black-and-white *Corian* dining table is surrounded by vintage Paul McCobb spindle-backed chairs. **Following spread:** Louis Poulsen pendants hang over the kitchen island with four vintage barstools. Haenisch replaced the existing island countertop with white marble and stained the wood a dark mahogany. **Pages 28–29, from left to right:** A custom mural designed by Haenisch adorns the playroom toy storage, which dialogues with the blue geometric *ZB Miletus* carpet from Stark; a Vik Muniz work embellishes the stairwell.

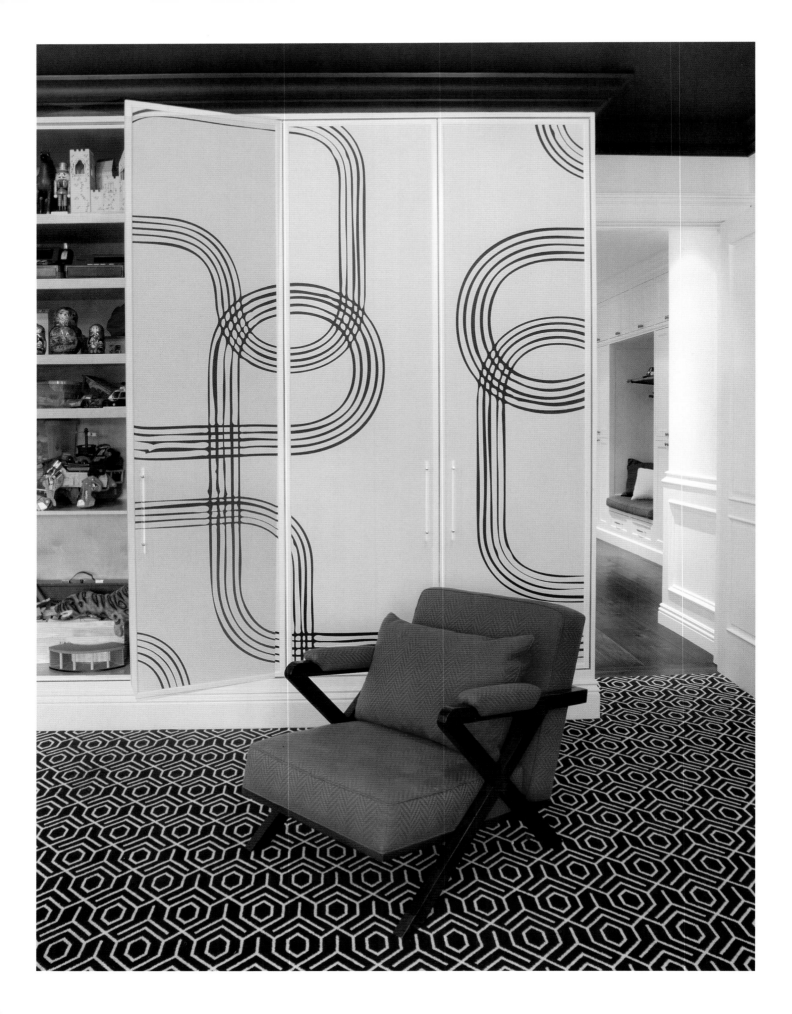

Previous spread: Master bedroom. A pair of vintage 1930s Italian industrial pendants were reworked into sconces and hang over the custom brass and lacquered wood nightstands flanking the custom linen-upholstered bed. The custom silk rug brings plush texture. *Night Writing* by Teresita Fernández hangs above the vintage étagère and Desa lamp from Ligne Roset. **Above:** Master bedroom seating area. The *Tinga* ceramic floor lamp is by Tahir Mahmood. Haenisch resized and reupholstered the client's existing sofa to fit the curve of the bay window, and also repurposed their former entry fixture into the master bedroom chandelier.
Opposite: Master bathroom. Galbraith & Paul wallpaper, a custom mirror, and vintage Italian sconces from Obsolete make for an elegant statement.

HOLLYWOOD
HILLS

While the interior and exterior materials of this 1959 modern home needed updating, Haenisch was instantly attracted to its well-proportioned spaces and the natural beauty of the site. Situated on a knoll and protected by a canopy of forty-foot-tall pine trees, the property demonstrated a playfulness, an "architectural funkiness" that he wanted to explore and accentuate. The house, which Haenisch occupies, has become a bit of a laboratory for his design practice. In addition to being a place for him to experiment with fabrics, colors, and furnishings that he later incorporates into his work for others, the home has become a testing ground for Haenisch's ability to infuse his design work with a sense of humor: a place to explore the dynamics of introducing the whimsical and unexpected, like the oversized lifeguard chair that commands attention poolside or the "sheep" standing in attention in the dining area. In this regard, the space has become both a sanctuary and playground for Haenisch.

The flooring, both inside and out, was terracotta tile, which in the interior was replaced by random natural oak. Haenisch had the newly installed oak wire brushed before it was finished to enhance its texture. Knotty pine interior walls were painted white, as Haenisch was not a fan of the knots in the wood but did want to maintain the texture of the paneling. The palette was intentionally kept quite neutral with pools of color coming from artwork and objects. Haenisch wanted the spaces to feel light, happy, and informal and he hoped to create the vibe of a modernized bungalow. To help accomplish this, he opened the kitchen to the living room by adding a counter and stools. The pool and deck area had been covered in Spanish tiles, which were removed and replaced with simple concrete with an exposed aggregate, again pared-back and textural. He also landscaped with agave and fichus hedges and then covered the knoll with an ivy groundcover, which is fluid, simple, and clean.

With white walls, neutral wood floors, and expanses of glass left unadorned as to let as much of the view in as possible, Haenisch focused his attention on creating warmth and comfort through the use of textures and let the often-whimsical furnishings and art set the tone of this relaxed and playful environment. Covering a large 1970s-era B&B Italia Mario Bellini *Camaleonda* modular sofa in the plush fabric used on teddy bears, for example, while both harmonious and textural, also invites visitors to return to a very specific playful place of warmth and comfort.

Haenisch acknowledges that the house is small, but also admits that he uses every room—something he believes is a testimony to its success.

Page 35: Haenisch's son's bedroom. A Peter Beard collage hangs above the vintage console. **Previous spread:** Living room. A vibrant artistic expression comes to life through the *Camaleonda* sofa by Mario Bellini upholstered in teddy bear fabric; Mona Kuhn's photograph *Refractions* over the mantle; *Dream Big* by Archie Scott Gobber above the television; Roger Capron's ceramic and metal fauna flanking the firebox; and Roger Shimomura's *Kansas Samurai Ed. 46* at the end of hallway. **Above:** Living room. An Eero Aarnio *Tomato* chair, *Bong* occasional table from Cappellini, *Oops* painting by Graham Gillmore, and a vintage acrylic chair forge an eclectically modern style. **Opposite:** Charter bar stools from Summit Furniture flank the kitchen counter. **Following spread, from left to right:** A trio of artworks enliven this living room wall: (from top) *Portrait of a Wasp* by Ben Murphey, *Il Tuffo*, 1951, by Nino Migliori, and *Back Flip Paradise Cove*, 1987, by Herb Ritts; a Dupree bar cart in red leather by Eric Brand, a 1952 pair of hurricane shades by Fulvio Bianconi for Venini, and a bull's eye prototype table designed by Studio 65 from Gufram illustrate Haenisch's penchant for unique details.

Pages 42–43: Dining room. Poul Volther dining chairs and a large pendant light by Vico Magistretti for Oluce complement the vintage Holly Hunt dining table, while an Andy Warhol *Cow* print graces the wall. **Previous spread, from left to right:** Master bedroom. This *Ox Chair* by Hans Wegner evokes mid-century chic; the *Kristan Closed/ Kristan Open* diptych by Dara Friedman and a glass globe pendant from Venini unite above the bed, while a black tar teddy bear by Mattia Biagi (placed over a blue vinyl dot), *Coney Island Bather* photograph by Lisette Model on the right upper wall, and a vintage Moroccan rug underscore the eclectic style. **Opposite:** View of Benedict Canyon. The umpire chair is from Tectona.

Above: Pool deck. A tree trunk merges with a custom lampshade designed by Haenisch. **Opposite:** The poolside offers the perfect environment for an outdoors theater. **Following spread:** Master bedroom at night. On the left bedside table stands a portrait of Haenisch's son Jake by Herb Ritts, and on the right is a 1961 photograph of Elizabeth Taylor by Douglas Kirkland.

TROUSDALE
ESTATES

There was a huge building boom in Los Angeles in the 1960s and entire neighborhoods, like the Trousdale Estates section of Beverly Hills, were dedicated to modern, flat-roofed, single-story homes. Hundreds were built in Trousdale and, in reality, not many of them were the work of noted architects and even fewer of them were actually constructed in a manner that would even remotely meet today's standards. This home certainly fell into that unfortunate category. So while Haenisch was anxious to celebrate the mid-century nature of the home that had initially attracted his clients to it, it also became clear that the intervention had to move the home from vintage mid-century to fully functioning contemporary.

When his clients found the home, the original owner had occupied it since its construction some fifty years earlier. Much of the garden was overgrown, and what was not overgrown was home to an oddly-shaped pool that seemed to dominate every sightline out of the house. It was not until the back garden was cleared that Haenisch realized how expansive the space was and he set his intention on capitalizing on this large, open space that appeared to be walled in by the surrounding green hills. Haenisch's first gesture was to square off the swimming pool and move it to the rear of the property, at the base of the bordering hill. He then poured three small concrete pads on the near side of the pool and installed ample teak daybeds, of his own design, on each pad. A fourth pad was installed at the far side of the pool. For this area, he designed a fireplace, which he then flanked with two cabanas, one on either side. The newly created outdoor space provided a much-needed focal point and an inviting destination that can be seen from nearly every room in the house.

Haenisch found the basic lines of the house appealing and liked the simple, boxy, straightforward nature of the architecture, but explains that, "Whenever you do an update on a house it's all about deciding what you're going to keep, what you're going to get rid of, and what you might reinterpret." So, for instance, there were decorative screens dividing the entry foyer from the sunken living room. Haenisch and his clients understood the necessity of the division, but found the decorative screens demanded an adherence to a specific stylistic moment that they were uninterested in perpetuating. Haenisch then came up with the notion of using slanted wood beams in a vertical repetition to create a sort of open barrier that provided views into the space while establishing the necessary corridor. The wood also added some much-needed warmth and a solid feeling to the space. The fenestration was also updated, which meant that simple sliding glass doors could be replaced by walls of fully retractable glass, establishing an indoor/outdoor flow that architects could only dream of some fifty years ago.

The kitchen was originally a small, closed off space with little access to the outdoors or family room. Haenisch opened the kitchen up to the living space and also created a pass-through bar with a counter and stools on the outside. The gesture was more in keeping with the casual entertaining the new owners hoped to do and the end result was a space that Haenisch hoped would be fun to be in.

We have seen all things mid-century elevated in the past few decades regardless of their original quality. With this project, Haenisch attempted to retain the essence of this mid-century gesture, without creating a time capsule. The end result is a contemporary, highly functioning home that pays homage to its mid-century origins without being limited by them.

Previous page: The entry spotlights a Retna painting and bleached oak floors throughout. **Above and opposite:** Living room. A Jeff Koons *Puppy* vase flanks the spectacular book-matched fireplace, which Haenisch restored. He added collapsible doors throughout. A Damien Hirst photograph entitled *For the Love of God*, a *Monolith* side table in "Negro Marquina" from Kelly Wearstler, and cocktail tables from Camerich LA finish the space. **Following spread:** A curved Jean Royère sofa and armchair contrast against the verticality of oak columns.

Opposite: Dining room. The graphic pattern of Fornasetti's *Il Sole* wallpaper highlights the simplicity of the Knoll table and Møller chairs. **Above:** Haenisch contemporized the space with floor-to-ceiling oak columns. **Following spread:** Kitchen. There was plenty of room for this second island once Haenisch removed the wall separating the kitchen from the family room. Tom Dixon brass pendants hang over the island with the marble waterfall edge.

Above: Master bedroom. A long bench from Hermès accompanies
the custom linen velvet upholstered bed and custom oak nightstands.
Opposite: Master bathroom. A striking photograph of Brad Pitt by
Martin Schoeller hangs above the bathtub.

Above: Haenisch added the outdoor fireplace and reworked an oddly shaped swimming pool. "So now everywhere you are in the house, when you look outside, you see fire, and at night the flames reflecting in the pool create this really great effect," he says. Haenisch designed the custom teak daybeds with black-and-white bolsters in Sunbrella fabrics. **Opposite:** *Dillon* lounge chairs from Jasper Furniture reside within one of the two custom cabanas in Sunbrella fabric.

BEL AIR

Haenisch had designed a beach retreat for a couple a few years ago, and when they decided to establish a family home on a property they had acquired in Bel Air, the couple reached out to Haenisch along with Tryggvi Thorsteinsson of Minarc, a Santa Monica-based architectural firm, for the project.

The wife had longed for a traditional white brick house with black shutters since she was a child, and the site in Bel Air, with its expansive flat pad of land and the surrounding traditional homes in an array of styles, seemed like the perfect spot for the home she envisioned. So, the team of designer, architect, and client set out to demolish the existing structure on the property and create a new home for this young family. Haenisch found the corner lot to be beautiful and wanted the completed home to showcase the views while taking full advantage of the large, flat plot nestled into the hills of this rather tony neighborhood. To accomplish this, the house was situated as close to the corner established by the intersecting roads as possible, leaving the maximum amount of land in the back of the house. The team then positioned the swimming pool at the very far end of the property, thus increasing the flat pad and allowing for elongated views from the public rooms at the rear of the house.

Haenisch, working with the architect, understood that the home had to function on multiple levels. The couple wanted a well-appointed home for formal entertaining, complete with a wine room and an oversized dining room capable of hosting large groups. They also wanted a home that would simultaneously support their young family and offer the intimate, family-centric spaces they required. To accomplish this, the more formal spaces were clustered around the central hall, with living on one side and dining on the other and the kitchen, which is open to the family room, and the children's play room located beyond the dining room in a wing of the home that can be closed off from the formal spaces.

Haenisch uses both color and furnishings to establish these distinctly different spaces. Working with backgrounds of grays, beiges, and whites Haenisch introduced pops of color—his client is particularly fond of lemon yellow—to underscore a transition or change in function, or simply to provide light and contrast. In a powder room off the formal living room, for example, Haenisch upholstered the door in yellow leather and then used two different wallpapers inside that juxtapose each other in an interesting and dynamic way. In the more formal spaces, he mixes some of the client's collection of Biedermeier furnishings with modern and contemporary pieces, with much of the upholstery of his own design. Haenisch also designed the series of disc lights that illuminate the arched hallway, which runs the length of the dining room and connects the entry with the study and wine room beyond.

In the kitchen and family room, Haenisch continues to use yellow: here it is paired with gray and the mix of traditional and modern furnishings effortlessly shifts from the more formal Biedermeier to farmhouse. Yellow accents shift to purple and grays in the master bedroom, but the mix of modern, contemporary, and antique continues to create an interesting dynamic.

Page 73: Entry. A sculpture by Guy Dill sits atop the "Nero Marquina" and "White Thassos" polished checkerboard floor. **Opposite:** Living room detail. A pair of Baguès-style gilt iron, tole, and rock crystal *bras de lumière* flank an Italian glass and gilt wood mirror. The pair of hide-upholstered *Leonine* stools are from Coup d'Etat. **Above:** Living room. A Michaël Verheyden white marble coupe sits atop a Nakashima walnut coffee table and between a pair of George Smith skirted linen swivel chairs and a Hollywood Regency-style sofa with bullion fringe. John Baldessari's *Warm Comfort from Prima Fascie* hangs above the mantle.

Opposite: Gallery. A row of custom brass ring chandeliers in a dark bronze finish hang from the groin-vaulted, Venetian-plastered ceiling. White oak wire-brushed floors in a natural finish are used throughout. **Above:** Dining room sitting area. A vintage *Egg* chair reupholstered in gray leather sits in front of a Biedermeier-style parcel ebonized fruitwood bookcase from Bonhams. A Joe Colombo *Birillo* bar stool stands next to the piano.

Dining room. A three-tier Murano glass foliage chandelier by Barovier & Toso hangs from a custom gilt Venetian-plastered ceiling by Agave Designs, and above a set of twelve George III–style fruitwood chairs from the late nineteenth century. The wall hosts a zoomorphic paint-decorated six-fold floor screen from the Doris Duke Collection.

Above: Kitchen. A pair of Coney Island pendants from Coup d'Etat hang above the island embellished with ice box latch-style hardware on the cabinet doors and a "Gray Mist" granite countertop. Custom colored tiles from Ann Sacks provide warmth to the backsplash. The breakfast table is custom zinc-wrapped. Haenisch stripped the finish on a set of Windsor chairs and refinished them to match the floor. **Opposite:** A Mary Corse painting hangs above the flagstone-clad fireplace, which is flanked by a *Power Play* Frank Gehry bentwood armchair. **Following spread:** Family room. The space comes alive with an oxidized brass linear tube *Compass* chandelier from Apparatus, a wingback armchair, a cut spiral Danish floor lamp from Ray Kisber Antiques, a chaise lounge, and a 1970s Laurel *Acorn* table lamp.
Pages 84–85, from left to right: The powder room door is upholstered in lemon yellow leather with a brass nailhead detail. A rock crystal fluted basin set from Sherle Wagner was installed on the nineteenth-century Louis-Philippe mahogany commode converted into the vanity. The wall lights are from Alberto Muselli Oggettistica, and the floor is a custom "Nero Marquina" and "White Thassos" honed basket weave mosaic; study. From the coffered ceiling hangs a multicolored Moravian star pendant from Mosaik. The rug from The Rug Company complements the custom slip-covered ottomans and Roman shade.

Previous spread: Master bedroom. Timeless elegance reigns via the large sixty-three-arm glass prism and metal *Sputnik* chandelier, Biedermeier commodes with rock crystal table lamps, the Holly Hunt *Sorraia* four-poster bed, a pair of Pierre Paulin chairs in mauve linen velvet next to the fireplace, and a stately Biedermeier center table on a custom area rug.
Opposite: Master bedroom. A *RAAK* Fuga wall light by Maija Liisa Komulainen highlights the fauteuil. **Above:** Master bathroom. A Roll & Hill teardrop wall light, a custom vanity, and a two-tiered brass chandelier with a fish motif from Tajan come together in the serene space.

SUNSET
ROUNDABOUT

This expansive apartment is located in a building that was designed by the architect Edward H. Fickett in the early 1950s, and Haenisch and his client were immediately drawn to the open space, views, and the unique character of the curvilinear architecture. The building is perched right above Sunset Boulevard and isn't very tall, but the hillside affords amazing views of the city and provides the sensation of being in the view, as opposed to above it. The building—a semi-circular form around an open, circular courtyard—did represent some challenges. Firstly, the curved form of the building meant that the radius defined many of the interior rooms, so furniture plans needed to be carefully considered to take advantage of the views, but also to make the most of the unconventional spaces. But the ever-present nature of the original architectural gesture also serves as a constant reminder that this is a piece of design, and many of the choices Haenisch made were to underscore that important distinction.

In order to bring warmth and charm into the big, open living space while unifying it to the rest of the apartment, Haenisch installed wide plank oak floors throughout. He also added a series of wooden beams to both diminish the "white box" quality of the apartment-house rooms and to render the space a bit more masculine and organic. The addition of wood on the floors and ceiling also infused the space with character that was lacking. Haenisch left the remainder of the backgrounds light.

He hoped that color would come from the art, furnishings, and objects, but did incorporate some Fornasetti wallpaper in the dressing area off the bedroom.

When it came to the furnishings, Haenisch wanted to put together an eclectic mix that would stand out from the building's creative construction and celebrate it without being forced into a narrow early-1950s stylistic vein. He accomplished this with a wild assortment of furnishings as diverse and distinct as the chairs by Jean Royère and Wendell Castle, which are peppered around the loft-like space. Haenisch also designed a series of black ceiling fixtures that look like inverted umbrellas. He also took a Noguchi paper lantern, covered part of it with black tar, and hung it from a rope. This construction became the much-loved dining room chandelier. Drapery was also used, not on the windows, but rather to frame and distinguish the dining area from the living area. The beige, black, and white linen add both color and texture and soften the space.

While the apartment is not as large as some of the homes Haenisch has designed, he made real efforts to create distinct spaces that, he hoped, would foster different experiences. In an intimate den, for example, he ran the flooring up the walls to create an enveloping space that he believed would create a cocoon-like environment unique from that offered by the bright, window-lined main living room.

139813
C LEVELAND
32 5'8 126
NOV 3 1970
Jean Prouvé
wolterinck's world OUT|IN

Page 91: Dining room. A Noguchi lamp with hand-painted black paint drips hangs over a Martin Visser table surrounded by Edward Wormley chairs. **Previous spread:** Living room. The Jean Royère maple-framed daybed was upholstered in goat fur. Haenisch added the architectural beams and custom ceiling fixtures to the interior. **Opposite:** Living room. Tom Friedman and Gustavo Godoy sculptures sit below Russell Young's *Hanoi Jane* screen print. **Above:** Haenisch added antlers to the papier-mâché moose head hanging in the bar.

Opposite: Living room. A 1961 ash stand by Estelle & Erwin Laverne stands next to the campaign-style metal daybed by Piero Fornasetti. The custom black demi-globe pendants were designed by Haenisch. **Above:** A pair of fiberglass lounge chairs by Wendell Castle surround a John Keal for Brown-Saltman checkerboard top walnut coffee table. Haenisch designed the custom striped linen drapes. **Following spread:** Kitchen. Haenisch designed the oak cabinetry, and the industrial pendant lights are from CB2.

Foyer looking into the family room. On the left hangs a KAWS painting of Sponge Bob. A 1970s upholstered ottoman by Mario Bellini sits below a Denis Darzacq print. Haenisch added a porthole to the door on the right for a whimsical touch.

Opposite: Master bedroom. Photographs by Ryan Holden Singer hang above the bed, which is comprised of a Nakashima walnut slab headboard.
Above: In an alcove adjacent to the master bath, Fornasetti and floral wallpaper create an eye-popping contrast, while a George Hurrell photograph of Veronica Lake sits above a custom dresser by Haenisch.

BEL AIR
COUNTRY CLUB

Haenisch had been hired to design the interiors of this traditional, shingle-style home by its previous owners and when they sold the home to an actor and his family, Haenisch was recommended and later given the chance to revisit the property and continue working on it for its new owners.

Working on the same home for two distinct clients presented Haenisch with a unique opportunity: there were things from the first renovation that did not make their way into the project, such as modernizing the space by enhancing the flow between the indoors and the out—something that can be tricky in classic homes. Haenisch and his new client were drawn to the home's traditional feel, however that also meant smaller, closed-off rooms and limited access to the outdoors. The main objective here became striking a balance between reviving the home and maintaining its conventional vibe and roots. At the same time, Haenisch's clients were interested in contemporary, vintage, and time-honored design, so perusing an eclectic mix of furnishings became part of the mandate.

In order to facilitate his new client's dream of Southern California indoor/outdoor living, Haenisch added a series of doors to the "barn room," a casual family area adjacent to the breakfast room. Here he also added a stone fireplace and wood paneling in an attempt to warm the space up while simultaneously making it feel as if it were part of the outdoors. Outside the barn room, Haenisch added a fire pit, which provides a visual extension of the living space and offers unparalleled views of the city below.

The traditional scale of the home also meant that many of the rooms were small. Opening them up to the exterior was one way of mitigating this experience. However, when it came to the kitchen, Haenisch decided to open it up to the family room, thus creating a large, casual space with easy access to the outdoors. Here, he replaced the kitchen island with a wooden piece that was designed to look as if it were an extension of the floor, and used white marble for the countertop. On the perimeter he incorporated white cabinetry and gray countertops—a gesture Haenisch hoped would make the island feel more like a piece of furniture, and thus connect the space to the family room beyond.

The house also offered the opportunity to design specific rooms for specific members of the family: a poker room was established for the husband, his and hers bathrooms for husband and wife, and a playroom for the children. Haenisch ran with this and infused each of these spaces with a personal identity. The poker room hosts a custom poker table, wool plaid curtains, and wood paneling. In the husband's bathroom and dressing area he covered the walls with a masculine, wool paperbacked fabric, installed lockers from the French Campaign Period, an eighteenth-century chest of drawers, a Moroccan rug, and a California contemporary chair.

Throughout the home, Haenisch mixes furnishings and objects from diverse periods and places, a gesture that certainly renders the home less formal. But it is his architectural intervention here that has successfully provided this traditional home with a sense of modern ease.

Page 105: Living room detail. A leather armchair from Jean de Merry sits before the bookcase from Mecox. **Previous spread:** Living room. A variety of pieces make for an exotic statement: custom sofas covered in velvet, Danish *Ox Art* ceramic cocktail tables, a *Tinted Lens* side table from Holly Hunt, floor lamp from Waldo's Designs, and a kilim ottoman from Horchow. **Above:** Living room detail. A pair of circa 1940 vintage Austrian armchairs surround the round iron center table from Lucca Antiques, which hosts a table lamp from Hollywood at Home. **Opposite:** Breakfast room. Chairs by Hollywood at Home accompany the dining table from Paul Ferrante.

Previous spread: Kitchen. Vintage style with modern accents comes through in the barstools from Hollywood at Home, the reclaimed wood island with a Carrara marble counter, the pot rack from Ann-Morris, perimeter countertops and backsplash in Basaltina stone, and floors in French oak. **Opposite:** Dining room. The nineteenth-century dining table from Lucca Antiques, custom chandelier, and paperbacked fabric on the walls from Hollywood at Home evoke a traditionally elegant feel. **Above:** Barn. A cozy atmosphere is established through the flagstone-clad chimney, vintage exercise bench with a leather top (used as the coffee table), a nineteenth-century French architect lamp from Obsolete, and the *Beni Ouarain* carpet from Jamal's Rug Collection.

Above: Home office. The mix of a custom-designed poker table and light pendant, *Durance* wall cabinet by Bourgeois Bohème Atelier, plaid alpaca drapery fabric, and Eames *Aluminum Group* office chairs by Herman Miller capture the home's vintage allure. **Opposite:** Playroom. The *La Mela* print by Enzo Mari, Danish farm table – which Haenisch had painted in a checkerboard pattern, and eighteenth-century French benches exemplify the house's diverse furnishings.

Above: Her master bathroom. An airy, feminine vibe is achieved through paperbacked fabric on the walls and custom George Smith armchairs. **Opposite:** His dressing room. A vintage chair from Paul Marra Design, vintage French campaign lockers from Bourgeois Bohème, a rug from Lawrence of La Brea, and paperbacked fabric on the walls reinforce the space's masculine style.

Opposite: Poolside loggia. The breezy, outdoor space is punctuated by a flagstone pool deck, Sutherland lounge chairs, and hurricanes from Formations. **Above:** Trellis-covered patio. The custom armchairs and slip-covered stools are by Haenisch. Christian Liaigre crafted the side tables.

PARK
CITY

When Haenisch's Los Angeles–based clients decided to build a mountaintop vacation home in Park City, Utah, they were sure to tap into Haenisch's resources. His clients chose the Boulder, Colorado, architecture firm of DTJ Design and charged them with the task of building a modern home that would be appropriate for the spectacular mountain setting, while also taking advantage of the magnificent mountain views. Haenisch was able to meet with the architects as the home was being planned and built, and helped direct the creation of the interior spaces. Having already worked with this client and maintaining first-hand knowledge of how they use and enjoy their home, he was a perfectly informed liaison between client and architect.

The home was designed around a main living room with high, pitched ceilings and dramatic views of the mountains in the distance. Here, Haenisch incorporated rough-hewn wood beams, which underscore the ceiling's gesture and add warmth to the space. Wide plank oak floors and a stacked stone fireplace add a sense of drama while calling to mind the home's fantastic natural setting. Haenisch also left the window and door frames in natural wood as yet another reminder of the abundant nature beyond the confines of the home. In the living room Haenisch integrated a bold, striped fabric on a daybed that he designed and placed at the center of the long narrow room, dividing the dining and living areas. Here, the custom daybed introduces the notion of complete relaxation as well as the colors Haenisch used for the remainder of the upholstery. The yellow, blue, and red that is

used throughout the room all stem from the striped fabric on the daybed. For this space Haenisch also designed a massive hanging chandelier in wood, rope, and hand-blown glass that hangs over the daybed. Additionally, he conceived of the shaded floor lamp with a swing arm that hovers above the dining table. The custom-designed lamp is on a swivel and wheels, so it adds a playful, interactive quality. Haenisch wanted this interior to be comfortable, inviting, and feel warm and he accomplished this by mixing traditional, antique, and modern furnishings together with modern art. In the living room, a mid-century Scandinavian tile-topped coffee table comingles with an antique painted faux bois chest of draws flanked by two vintage chairs with rush seats and sides that have been painted blue.

Haenisch also opened the kitchen up into the main room by paneling the entire space so that the kitchen would maintain its own identity, but still merge with the living area. Then, he incorporated a mix of nineteenth-century painted furniture and a vintage industrial cart and laboratory stools.

Throughout the home, Haenish aimed to infuse the space with surprise and whimsy and a certain amount of levity. In the master bedroom, for example, he designed the bed with a leather headboard and faux bois posts. In the children's bunkroom, the bunk beds were constructed from actual tree trunks and bold colors were used to reinforce the notion of fun. Haenisch hoped the dynamic, natural, and engaging surroundings of the home would foster indelible memories for this family.

Previous page: Entry. A curved back sofa from Denmark 50, a marquetry game table from Revival Antiques, and a kilim ottoman from Horchow all capture the home's mountain setting. **Above:** Great room. Haenisch used pops of color, especially red, throughout and convinced the client to go with a light blond finish on the floors, doors, windows, and ceiling beams. A pair of yellow linen lounge chairs effortlessly contrast with the blue linen sofa, all custom-made and designed by Haenisch. **Opposite:** The antler-legged stool sits next to a vintage Danish tile table and on top of a *Squiggle Orange* rug from The Rug Company. The vintage floor lamp is from Hollywood at Home. **Following spread, from left to right:** This space hosts a custom rope-wrapped chandelier above the tête-à-tête daybed, and a Guido Gambone bull sculpture that sits on a nine-teenth-century Spanish chest.; in the dining area, a custom over-scaled floor lamp hangs over the custom oak dining table by Haenisch. The art is by S. B. Landau Photography.

Previous spread: Kitchen. An abundance of wood underscores the home's natural inspiration: the custom Shaker-style cabinetry is in knotty alder wood and the hardware is a *Mayfair Cup Pull* and *Mushroom Knob* in rust from Top Knobs; the *Carlyn Double Pendant* is from The Urban Electric Co.; the vintage French industrial bar cart through Cleveland Art inspired the design of the island topped with Carrara marble.
Opposite: Three handwoven lounge chairs by John Himmel through David Sutherland surround a custom table by Haenisch. The driftwood chandelier is from Dan Marty and the *Bryant* sconces from Circa Lighting.

Previous spread: Bunk room. The colorful custom carpet from Stark and *Number* chairs from Eurotrend bring a bold playfulness to the room, which also features La Lune Collection bunk beds. **Above:** Powder room. Roberto Dutesco's photograph *Love Bite*, a superordinate antler sconce from Roll & Hill, and a hand lamp and vanity sconces from Interieurs nod to the natural setting, while the blue cross medicine cabinet from Cappellini and the red Haenisch-designed custom round wall mirror add pops of color. **Opposite:** Bunk room bathroom. Haenisch chose a blond barn wood for the walls and cabinetry.

Opposite: Guest bedroom. A harmonious interplay of blue and red hues is seen in the vintage toy fire truck from Cabin Fever Antiques sitting atop the vintage chest of drawers, and the circa 1940s blue armchair from Denmark 50. **Above:** Guest bedroom. The inviting space features a Burton Morris *Taxi* serigraph, a pair of Jens Risom nightstands, a *Brasa* floor lamp from Ikea, and an *Akari* light sculpture from the Noguchi Museum.

Above: Master bedroom. Many of the furnishings evoke the textures and colors of the view outdoors, such as the faux-bois iron canopy bed with a leather headboard designed by Haenisch, nightstands from Eric Brand, and a wing-back chair.
Opposite: Master bathroom. A pair of Massimo Vitali prints and a vintage chain chandelier hang above the bathtub.

MALIBU
SHORE

When Haenisch's client purchased this house, it was originally four disjointed buildings scattered across a fantastic plot of land, high above the beach in Malibu. The property offers a great deal of privacy, which can often mean that it is closed in and walled off from the world, but its expansive views of the ocean provide the site with an openness to the world that is hard to come by.

Haenisch was hired, and together with his client they came up with a plan to unify the various buildings and transform the site into a functioning home. Their goal focused on the idea of creating a compound and providing all the buildings with a common vocabulary of materials and intention so that they would appear as if they were built at the same time. The architect Michael Kovac was brought in to work with the client and Haenisch on the main house.

Haenisch was keen on organizing the space so that a sense of arrival occurred upon entering the property as opposed to entering the front door of the main house. In order to accomplish this, he focused his attention on entering and experiencing the compound. He gated the entire property and positioned the gate door, which he wanted to feel like a "front door" notwithstanding the fact that it was outside, in such a way as to offer unobstructed views of the ocean as soon as you open the door and glance into the compound.

Haenisch's client longed for a welcoming home suitable for both the casual entertaining of larger groups, but also for an intimate, private retreat. The various buildings allowed for this sort of expansion and contraction: when one or two people use the home, it feels comfortable and appropriate, and there isn't a sense of the vast emptiness that can occur in a single, large home. When there are guests, the other buildings can be used. An informal appreciation of the very special site became the guiding force behind many of the decisions that were made. And notwithstanding the tony Malibu location, Haenisch understood that his client was not looking for rigid, formal spaces but rather hoped that the compound would embrace the spectacular nature of the ocean-side location with easy, welcoming gestures. With this in mind, Haenisch set out to transform the buildings and established a narrative based on the notion that they were once a series of old barns that had been remodeled and converted into this residential compound. He ran many of his choices through this narrative and if they passed the test, he knew he was on target. In keeping with these goals, horizontal paneling was used to clad the exterior, which was then painted a dark charcoal, and random stone was used both inside and outside the main house and for the guesthouse.

When it came to the interior spaces, Haenisch's client wanted everything to be calm and easy on the eye, so he incorporated grays and whites and introduced a bit of blue from the ocean, making efforts to keep it subdued. Haenisch designed much of the upholstery and peppered the house with some of the design objects his client loves to collect, like the Ettore Sottsass ceramics and Jacques Adnet bookshelf.

Previous page: Living room detail. A Jacques Adnet étagére, Kent Williams painting, and an *Eclipse* steel table lamp by Jose Esteves from Interieurs forge a harmonious statement. **Above:** Guest House. The *Love, Love, Love* painting by Matthew Heller, vintage Pollock *Executive Chairs*, and poured concrete floor reinforce the home's pared-back style. **Opposite:** Living room. The gray and white palette makes itself evident through the flagstone fireplace surround, vintage French architects' floor lamp, Hans Wegner armchair, and parchment and steel cocktail table.

Previous spread: Kitchen sitting room. The space evokes the ocean-side location through casual furnishings: a custom sofa and armchairs by Haenisch, stools by Paul McCobb, a cocktail table by Rodolfo Dordoni from Minotti, a Christian Liaigre floor lamp, a pashmina wool rug from The Rug Company, and a photograph by Massimo Vitali. **Above:** Kitchen. Mosler *Grande Acrylic* pendant from Nessen Lighting, Caesarstone quartz countertops in "Blizzard," and vintage barstools all contribute to the simple yet elegant atmosphere. **Opposite:** Screening house's galley kitchen. "It's become one of the most popular spots at the compound. The space started out as an office with a galley kitchen and felt very closed off," says Haenisch, who opened it up by adding "hot dog" windows. "I call them that because they open up and out, like the windows on food trucks, and it's now become the hub for Sunday parties—there's a bartender and a chef."

Opposite: Powder room. The mirror is custom made by Haenisch and the WaterBridge Premium Designer Faucet is from Sonoma Forge.
Above: Master bedroom's sitting room. A custom daybed, a painting by Matt Palmer, an *Avalon* cashmere throw by Hermès, and a pashmina rug from The Rug Company create the relaxing environment.

Master bedroom. The gray and white palette with hints of blue continues through smoked French oak floors, a custom bed made in zinc by CAC Fabrication, selenite-topped iron nightstands from Blackman Cruz, *Chesterfield* wool rugs from DDC, a two-tone swag leg chair by George Nelson, and a vintage *Ion* desk chair by Gideon Kramer.

Master bathroom. Honed gray pearl onyx countertops and shower walls, ebonized white oak cabinetry and mirror frame by Martin & Carter, *Easton Classic* sink fittings in matte nickel by Waterworks, custom pendant lights, and a chair and ottoman upholstered in velvet complete the spa-like space.

Above: The breezy outdoor space is defined by a John Lautner concrete round table paired with concrete stools and *Inout 09* teak lounge chairs by Paola Navone from Gervasoni. **Opposite:** A Paola Lenti float chaise lounge and a poolside sofa and coffee table from Sutherland Furniture elicit relaxed sophistication. **Following spread:** Ipe decking, a custom-made banquette, and a teak and steel lava rock fire pit make for the perfect ocean-side hangout.

BEVERLY
HILLS

Haenisch's client, a single mother of two with a passion for all things equestrian, sought out the designer to transform this neglected mid-century traditional house into a fully functioning home with an abundance of character. The space had experienced decades of differed maintenance, and parts of it seemed more dated than others. Haenisch quickly realized that the classic parts of this home—the divided light windows, the progression and order of the rooms, and scale of the spaces—still read as traditional, however all the home's functioning aspects, like the kitchen and baths, were not only dated but also seemed out of place, as they, too, closely referenced the home's mid-century origins.

Haenisch set out to celebrate the historic aspects of the home while making certain it would function for this family. In addition to meeting their needs, the new owner hoped the home would reflect her interest in both traditional and modern design, as well as her passion for riding without becoming excessively masculine. To meet these goals, new flooring, fireplaces, roof, kitchen, and baths were designed and installed. In addition, the upper floor—dedicated to the bedrooms—was reorganized so it would provide two sizable rooms for the children and a master suite instead of the collection of smaller bedrooms that existed.

Wide plank oak floors with an open grain were chosen for the majority of the living spaces, while the original terracotta tiles were kept in the sunroom. In this dramatically windowed space, Haenisch added paneling, which was then painted white. Paneling was also brought into the master bedroom and new mantels were designed and placed in both the living and master bedroom. A pair of bookcases that flank a nearly floor-to-ceiling window in the living room were added and the ceiling in this room was painted in a light blue

color. Haenisch and his client were not afraid of color: the equestrian-themed bar incorporates a deep olive; the powder room, another homage to all things equestrian, is an assemblage of Hermès wallpapers in their classic orange; and the butler's pantry, which Haenisch opened to the kitchen, was painted in a deep indigo. Bright, colorful, yet traditional wallpaper was also used in the dining room and a bold plaid fabric that complements the deep olive was used to cover part of the walls in the bar.

When it came to the furnishings, Haenisch and his client were often drawn to the traditional, as can be seen in the dining room. However, some important modern pieces were also incorporated. A pair of Guillerme et Chambron chairs, for example, commands attention in the sunroom atop a rug of Haenisch's own design. Haenisch also designed the rugs in the living room and bar. A vintage rug was purchased for the master bedroom and provides a backdrop for the bed, which is in faux bamboo. Here, Haenisch designed an ample chaise lounge that seamlessly mixes with the other antiques while providing a relaxing perch.

Like the house, the property offered many opportunities to develop specific spaces and Haenisch and his client were not afraid to let them exist independently. Rooms shift from indigo to orange to olive without feeling disjointed or out of place. This provides the home with a casual, relaxed, yet elegant feel. The interiors are filled with elements of surprise and discovery as opposed to a singular direction established by the color or style of some overreaching design theme. Similarly, the terraced, hillside property also provides distinct spaces. A flat patio area exists off the living area, and upon climbing up some stairs one encounters the guesthouse and swimming pool, and after continuing to climb the tennis court is revealed, none of which is visible from inside.

Page 161: Entry. Historical inspiration is evident in the natural fiber wall covering combined with an Empire-style gilt metal portico clock, a pair of Louis XVI gilt bronze candlesticks, an *Emilio Rock Console* base from Hollywood at Home with a custom oak top, and the *Tatham* wall lights from Jamb. **Pages 162–163, from left to right:** A Bobbin chair with natural rush and a Peter Duhman *Bukhara* throw pillow from Hollywood at Home stands in front of the stairway; Haenisch refinished the client's existing console to match the new white oak floors that he incorporated throughout. The photograph is *Elephant Train* by Nick Brandt, the pair of table lamps are by Natan Moss. **Previous spread:** Living room. Classic elegance reigns through the various furnishings: a custom lounge chair and ottoman, which sits underneath a framed silk scarf entitled *Le Pégase d'Hermès*; a circa 1960s Sori Yanagi for Tendo Mokko oak coffee table pairs with a custom sofa; brass *Dean Picture* lights from Circa Lighting hanging above the custom-designed built-in bookcases; a Paul László mirror-top coffee table and flanked by a pair of 1940s Gilbert Rohde–inspired lounge chairs in 8" bullion fringe; a custom sofa, a brass cone floor lamp from Dana John; and custom wool rugs.

Above and opposite: Powder room. Wallpapers from Hermès cover the walls, while a custom-pleated linen treatment embellishes the octagonal window. A circa 1950s Heritage Henredon Dorothy Draper *Espana* stool complements the orange and brown palette.

Above and opposite: Sunroom. The light-filled space features a
circa 1970 pair of Guillerme et Chambron oak armchairs; a custom
sofa; and a mica-veneered mahogany coffee table in the manner
of Samuel Marx (which was also selected for the Oval Office during
the Obama administration).

Previous spread: Dining room. A vintage long-arm brass pendant from Collected by Jason Koharik hangs over the mid-nine-teenth-century Louis-Philippe walnut dining table paired with William IV mahogany dining chairs. A 1970s Guillerme et Chambron credenza and an 1820s Regency plinth sitting in the bay window add to the space's traditional style. **Above:** Kitchen. The custom floors are a combination of marble and granite in "Negro Marquina," "Calacatta Gold," and "Blue Bahia." Haenisch powder-coat-ed a pair of vintage pendants in white to hang over the island, which he covered in reclaimed wood. **Following pages, from left to right:** Breakfast room. Haenisch designed a custom banquette around the early-twentieth-century French table. He added a pair of eighteenth- and nineteenth-century mismatched Windsor chairs. A Jacques Garcia *Couronne Chandelier* from Baker hangs from the beams that Haenisch incorporated to highlight the A-frame ceiling; kitchen detail. The countertops and backsplash are in "Calacatta Gold." **Pages 180–181:** Haenisch added solid oak wood paneling on the walls and ceiling in the master bedroom for texture and warmth. The vintage rug reinforces the color palette. The bed and matching nightstand are in custom faux bamboo, and an embroidered Indian throw from Hollywood at Home is at the foot of the bed. **Pages 182–183, from left to right:** Haenisch incorporated a dressing table in the master closet niche with a vintage Ruhlmann makeup chair. A vintage pair of tulip sconces from Liz's Antique Hardware flank a *Trumeau Mirror* from Jasper Furniture; master bathroom. A circa 1840 English mahogany chest with ivory escutcheons and silver pulls sits between a pair of custom polished nickel sink vanities and mirrors. A set of four *Clandon Storm* wall lights in brass are from Vaughan, and the Scandinavian rug is from Jamal's Rug Collection.

MALIBU
HILLS

Haenisch had previously collaborated with this client when he was called in to personalize this Malibu Hills home and infuse it with new life. The client had worked with the Venice-based architect Lewin Wertheimer on this meticulously constructed, shingle-style traditional house but never moved in. Instead, the newly completed home was rented out and it was not until some four years later that Haenisch's client decided to take possession of the home, have Haenisch complete the interiors, and move in with his family.

While Wertheimer's design provided Haenisch with well proportioned, appropriately scaled rooms and a working arrangement and sequence of spaces, the home felt generic, as it was never fully customized for its owner. Haenisch set out to infuse the house with character and transform it from a blank slate into a warm and welcoming reflection of the kind of life his clients envisioned.

Sitting on an ample piece of land in the hills above the Pacific Ocean, this home offers spectacular views of the water and majestic sunsets over the Pacific. In addition to exquisite moldings and architectural details made with the highest quality materials, Wertheimer provided the large house with many opportunities to enjoy the view. It then became Haenisch's goal to make those details and unique materials come to life, and make certain that those spaces were not only used, but were also enjoyed to their full potential.

Haenish's imprint is experienced as soon as one enters the home. In the soaring foyer, for example, he installed gray wallpaper, which softens the space, but more importantly provides the beautiful moldings and trim with the contrast they required to subtly shine. This space underscores the efforts that went into building this traditional home and sends a clear message that it's a highly considered environment. Haenisch also covered the walls of the adjacent dining room in a paperbacked fabric. Here, he added a massive Scandinavian dining table, a traditional chandelier, an antique server, and covered the chairs in indigo and white fabrics. The kitchen, just beyond the dining room, opens on to the family room and breakfast room. In the breakfast room, which is lined with a collection of blue and white dinnerware and serving pieces, Haenisch incorporated more Scandinavian chairs, this time modern and vintage, and designed the banquette for the space. The adjacent family room hosts custom upholstery of Haenisch's own design, including a round ottoman and a custom round rug with border, again in tones of blue as pulled from the ever-changing spectacle of blue and gray that exists outside the many windows.

A fan of providing visual access between the spaces he designs, Haenisch had ample opportunity to play with such access, as much of the ground level exists off a very wide common hallway. The kitchen, pantry, family room, and breakfast room all dwell as a large, open expanse, yet the architectural details and the furnishings provide them with a certain amount of autonomy.

The lower level hosts a gym and a state-of-the art screening room. While the rest of the home seems to take its chromatic cues from the ocean and sky, Haenisch wanted to tap into the glamorous days of movie-going for the screening room. Here, an elegant red is paired with black and gold to create a style that is certainly unique within the home and accentuates the idea of escape that is behind the cinematic experience.

Page 185: Entry. An eighteenth-century Portuguese red-painted chest and a vintage camelback settee bring lively color. **Pages 186–187:** Living room. *Sidewalk* by Andy Warhol, a circa 1960 La Gardo Tackett fish plate on the coffee table, Katie Leede throw pillows on a custom linen upholstered sofa, and an ebonized *Bobbin* chair from Formations enliven the space. **Previous spread:** Living room. A custom parchment-topped mahogany coffee table sits beneath a leather and brass chandelier from Apparatus. A late nineteenth-century bench, custom sofa, armchairs, and daybed complete the space. On the walls, a pair of twig sconces from Vaughan, a Sugimoto *Stanford Theatre* gelatin silver print, and a Damien Hirst kaleidoscope print are hung together. **Above:** Dining room. The dining set is Gustavian-style, and a Henri Cartier-Bresson gelatin silver print hangs over the mantle. **Opposite:** A circa 1840 English sideboard stands beneath a circa 1860 English gilded mirror. The walls are dressed in a paperbacked stripe.

Opposite: Family room. The custom ottoman is upholstered in a Yao hill tribe linen. A pair of rolled-back *Rive Gauche* armchairs from Hollywood at Home stand on a custom round wool rug designed by Haenisch. **Following spread:** In the break-fast room Haenisch darkened the finish on these vintage Kai Kristiansen *Compass* teak dining chairs to blend with the dark floors. The chairs sit opposite the custom channeled banquette.

Previous page: Master bedroom. The *Arch Top Chandelier* in bronze is by E. F. Chapman.
Above, opposite, and following spread: Screening room. A Jamie Johnson photograph
entitled *I Will Not Date Actors* hangs on a wall. The custom red wool carpet is from
International Flooring. The walls were upholstered to match the custom upholstered red
cotton velvet soft furnishings with a mustard cord trim. The coffee table is custom-made
in walnut with a bronze inlay. The pendant lights and sconces are by Jacques Garcia.

TROUSDALE
COLDWATER CANYON

The creator of *The Brady Bunch* and *Gilligan's Island* originally owned this flat-roofed, mid-century home. In its original state, it included a sunken family room, limited windows, a closed-off service kitchen, and expanses of terrazzo flooring. When its new owners approached Haenisch, they were interested in the home's potential and loved the privacy the site offered, but much of its mid-century appeal had faded beyond recognition and what was left simply didn't meet their needs.

Haenisch and his clients appreciated the simplicity of the existing architecture, which was free of unnecessary detail, and very much wanted to retain or accentuate all that made it modern while extracting it from the very specific moment of its early 1960s construction. In order to accomplish these goals, Haenisch set out to open the space up to the views and enhance the indoor-outdoor flow while infusing it with warmth. A collection of single-pane sliding doors that ran along the back of the home were replaced with state-of-the-art retractable floor-to-ceiling windows. When open, it's as if the entire rear-facing wall of the home were removed. This gesture clearly opened the interior spaces up to the view and each other, but also brought the expansive patio and pool into the house, creating the perception of one big room that extends out to include nearly all

of the flat outdoor space, master bedroom, living room, family room, and kitchen.

The same philosophy of breaking down the distinctions between indoors and out was applied to the interior divisions. Haenisch's vision for the home included an open kitchen, family room, and breakfast room, but it went further to disintegrate what he saw as the dated hierarchy. He felt no reason to maintain a formal living room with finer furnishings and an informal family room with more casual objects if these distinctions had nothing to do with the way his clients wanted to use the space. Instead, his vision for the home would neutralize the differences between the interiors and encourage a free-flowing use and appreciation of all of them. Perhaps it is this distinction that is at the core of the intervention here.

Haenisch wanted to underscore that the rooms, which together compose the living core of the home, were to be used interchangeably. He installed a vibrant oak floor throughout to facilitate this while providing the space with a sense of warmth. The furnishings were chosen and positioned to facilitate use and encourage interaction and enjoyment throughout the abode. Here, Haenisch mixes mid-century and contemporary furnishings with the same ease he applied to rethinking the home's base architecture.

Page 203: Entry. A Ben & Aja Blanc *Moon* light graces the ceiling. **Pages 204–205, from left to right:** Entry. A pair of 1950s Italian wingback chairs sit beneath the *IC* wall lights, which flank Alex Prager's *3:56am, Milwood Ave.* print. The vintage brass and marble console is from Hollywood at Home; view of the entry from the living room. A pair of *Hollister* chairs from Hollywood at Home, a ribbon stool from Cappellini, and a planter from Rolling Greens offer vibrant touches. **Pages 206–207:** Dining room. Custom swing doors with brass rivets introduce the space, which is embellished with a *Crying Girl* lithograph by Roy Lichtenstein and Nakashima dining chairs, a Guillerme et Chambron credenza, and a photograph by Carl Corey. **Previous spread:** Kitchen. Tom Dixon pendants, a pair of Platner barstools, custom white lacquered cabinetry, and Calacatta marble countertops and backsplash define the space's sleek elegance. **Opposite:** Dining/wine room, designed by Haenisch. A *Wall Light 265* by Paolo Rizzatto hangs over a Knoll dining table featuring a Fabio Maria Micucci handcrafted glass vessel from Ralph Pucci and Poul Volther oak chairs. **Above:** View of the breakfast room from the kitchen. The *Gnome* sculpture by Ottmar Hörl and *Dirty Habit* photograph by Graham Bromley bring artful style to the space.

Opposite and above: Living room. A variety of works create a lively statement. *3:14pm, Pacific Ocean* by Alex Prager hangs on the opposite wall. Above, a pair of Minotti chairs flank the Yves Klein table, which sits atop a *Tidal* rug from The Rug Company. The *Flashwood Pendant* is from Masiero, and Graham Gilmore's *Try Not to Live Up to All My Expectations* hangs behind a custom linen-upholstered sofa with a Banksy *NOLA* screen print on the left.

Above: Powder room. The RAAK sconces are custom powder-coated. **Following spread:** Master bedroom. The artistic flair continues with a pair of screen prints by Harland Miller; custom designed nightstands and bed; a *Split Light* rug from The Rug Company; a *Carre d'assise* bench from Hermès; custom linen drapery; and a *Puppy Vase* sitting beneath the Alex Prager print. **Pages 220–221:** The pool area highlights *Billow* lounge chairs from Sutherland and custom six-foot-round ottomans designed by Haenisch, who also incorporated the folding door system.

BEVERLY HILLS
FRANKLIN CANYON

Haenisch worked with architect C. J. Bonura on this large and complex compound. Originally, when the client purchased the property, a modest home had existed there for decades. While the existing structure was positioned to take advantage of the views, it was not until that home was torn down and the new structures went up that Haenisch, the client, and the architect had a full understanding of just how spectacular the vistas were. Positioned in the hills above Beverly Hills, the property offers panoramas of the city below with the downtown skyscrapers in the distance from one direction and views of Los Angeles's Westside all the way to the ocean on the other.

While it's technically one building, the property is a collage of spaces—both indoor and out—as well as spaces that can become either and create a boomerang along the road at the highest point of the premises. The main house hosts a magnificent entry, study, kitchen, screening room, and a collection of living, dining, and lounging spaces interrupted by a rhythm of concrete and stone structural columns that welcome fireplaces and serve to create islands of intimate space within the vast living area. A series of fully retractable, ceiling-to-floor window doors were installed along the view side of the home. The upper floor ushers in two distinct areas, each accessed by a different stairwell. One stair leads to the master wing and a second leads to a collection of private guest rooms.

The living space leads to a stairway that precedes a gallery-like corridor. One side of the corridor can be folded away, transforming the space into an art-filled covered garden path that connects the main house to the guesthouse. Along this area one encounters an outdoor bar-kitchen and dining pavilion perched above the pool. When sitting outside in this area, it actually feels as if you're in a room with art, which goes very far toward blurring the distinctions between indoors and out.

The guesthouse can function as an autonomous three-bedroom residence with a living area, kitchen, and dining space on the first floor and the bedrooms above. The expansive pool borders the far end of the property and it, too, is in a boomerang shape, but here it mirrors the building's footprint to create a flat, grassy yard. The pool, which is seen from nearly every room in the house, naturally became one of the remarkable parts of the property. In the evening, when it is lit, it bathes the entire structure in a watery glow, providing the entire space with an otherworldly quality.

Teak is used throughout the home in conjunction with charcoal black paneling, concrete, and a sea of gray, monotone limestone that was quarried in Italy and used on the floors, both inside and out. When it came to the furnishings, Haenisch wanted to underscore the contemporary nature of the architecture. In a city deeply enthralled by mid-century architecture and design, using new design seemed like a welcome respite from what is expected. By doing so, Haenisch hoped to keep the focus on the accomplishments of the architecture within which he was working.

Haenisch was also careful to create some distinct and unique experiences within the home, which risked feeling like a hotel without them. He paneled the library, added the skylight in the kitchen above a slatted wood "ceiling," created a unique island in the kitchen with marble and a live-edge wood surface, designed the bar with strips of teak that support another live-edge top, designed a wine storage area that can be see from both the master staircase and the living space, and gave the powder room a distinctive paneling with brass detailing. The same level of care and detail spills over into the screening room, which is complete with a candy bar.

Page 223: The main entry pivot door is in teak. **Previous spread:** Den. An *Atlan* arm-chair, a white lacquer and glass coffee table from Flexform, ceramic vessels on the coffee table and wall shelving by Ben Medansky, a *Ginger* leather desk chair with legs in a wenge finish, and a silk and wool rug from Holland & Sherry all contribute to the cozy atmosphere. An Ed Ruscha *Wall Rocket* lithograph hangs in the hallway. **Opposite:** Living room. Clean, modern style comes through via the pair of *Hug* chairs in Canaletto walnut from Giorgetti, a coffee table from B&B Italia, and a pair of *Luggage* armchairs from Minotti. **Above and pages 232–233:** Family room. A *Tufty Time* sofa, a pair of leather *Jensen* armchairs, a Paolo Piva *Area* table, and a pair of quilted leather poufs from Minotti complement the diverse materials and architecture of the space.

Above: Dining room. Leather and brushed steel Italian dining chairs accompany the *Tadeo* dining table from Walter Knoll. **Following spread:** Kitchen. A bevy of materials animates the space, demonstrated by a walnut live-edge slab floating atop the Statuario Venato Betogli marble countertop; "Sleek Concrete" from Caesarstone on the perimeter counters; bar stools from Walter Knoll and CB2; and Simon Pearce glass pendants.

Previous spread: Bar. The bar stools are crafted in "Janson" leather.
Above: The fully stocked candy bar on the back wall of the in-home
movie theater. **Opposite:** Theater bathroom. The floating countertop
and sink are in "Wildfire" granite.

Previous spread: Master bedroom. The headboard wall and bed platform are custom-made, accompanied by a pair of Molteni & Co. nightstands lacquered in chalk white. The leather chaise longue from B&B Italia sits next to a Piero Lissoni side table. The swivel chairs and coffee table are from Minotti, and the wool and silk rug from Holland & Sherry. **Above:** His master bathroom. The shower walls are made in "Bianco Seta" marble. **Opposite:** Wet bar. The "Ogassian Penta 3D" ceramic tiles in a metallic bronze from Ann Sacks add texture to the space. **Following spread:** Outdoor dining room. The powder-coated aluminum armchairs are from Janus et Cie. The teak outdoor seating group features a Ben Medansky ceramic planter.

Previous spread: Guest house living room. A pair of Italian *Metropolitan* and *Klee* armchairs sit with custom tree trunk cocktail tables. **Above:** Guest house kitchen. Tom Dixon *Melt Mini* pendants, "Bottega" gray leather bar stools from DWR, and a Gaggenau wall-mounted hood oven and cooktop create a modern statement. **Opposite:** Guest house dining room. The blue tones of the B&B Italia leather and aluminum dining chairs complement the rug from Holland & Sherry. **Following spread:** Guest house master bathroom. White "Thassos" and "Crystal Cielo" marble form the chevron pattern on the floors.

CREDITS

Pacific Palisades
Photographer, Grey Crawford
Landscape Designer, Inner Gardens

Hollywood Hills
Photographer, Richard Powers, Peden + Munk

Trousdale Estates
Photographer, Simon Berlyn
Developer, Hadi Halawani

Bel Air
Photographer, Grey Crawford
Architect, Tryggvi Thorsteinsson of Minarc Design
Landscape Designer, Greg Sanchez of GDS Designs

Sunset Roundabout
Photographer, Tim Street-Porter
Developer, Hadi Halawani

Bel Air Country Club
Photographer, Roger Davies
Landscape Designer, Greg Sanchez of GDS Designs

Park City
Photographer, Grey Crawford
Architect, DTJ Design

Malibu Shore
Photographer, Simon Upton
Architect, Michael Kovac of Kovac Design Studio
Landscape Designer, Coral Browning

Beverly Hills
Photographer, Richard Powers
Landscape Design, Green Tree Landscaping

Malibu Hills
Photographer, Richard Powers
Architect, Lewin Wertheimer
Landscape Design, Marny Randall

Trousdale Coldwater Canyon
Photographers, Richard Powers and Simon Berlyn
Developer, Hadi Halawani

Beverly Hills Franklin Canyon
Photographers, Peter Murdock and Simon Berlyn
Architect, C.J. Bonura of Bonura Building
Developer, John Saca

WITH GRATITUDE

You come into the world with nothing and you leave with nothing but life's experiences in between—the interactions with family, friends, lovers, mentors, teachers, collaborators, and clients—are what make it full.

This journey could never have happened alone. With great affection I want to sincerely thank:

My clients, who put their trust in me, who allowed me to collaborate and create their most personal of spaces. When it works it's magic!

My team of talented artisans, craftsmen, upholsterers, and painters who take my ideas and make them reality at the highest level.

The many talented architects and contractors with whom I have collaborated and contributed to my work. The many amazing magazine and book editors who have published my work.

The fantastic photographers with whom I've had the privilege of working and who helped in bringing this book to life.

Rizzoli, and especially Publisher Charles Miers, Associate Publisher Anthony Petrillose, and Editor Gisela Aguilar who worked so hard in creating this book. Thank you for your patience, understanding, and kindness throughout this process.

All the people, past and present, at Trip Haenisch and Associates who have brought their passion, creativity, professionalism, and enthusiasm to work on a daily basis.

Anthony Iannacci, my friend, my editor. He inspired me to do this project and has been there every step of the way with his fine eye and steady focus. There wouldn't be a book without you.

Carrie Hunt, my creative and inspired graphic designer, who created a beautiful visual narrative for this book.

Lauren Urband, my publicist and confidant. Thank you for your vision, trust, support, and advice over the years.

Kari Pohost, my "right hand," for your years of support, your humor, and keeping this project under control and moving forward.

Hadi Halawani, my former assistant and good friend, for his incredible talent, sense of calm, and sense of humor. He, and his partner Kevin Howells, are my development partners. Their light and loyalty in my life have meant so much.

Courteney Cox, who wrote a heartfelt and insightful foreword. You have been an amazing, supportive, and loving friend.

Waldo Fernandez, who was my partner for over twenty years. I learned so much from you and I'm incredibly grateful. Without your support I would have never been a designer.

Lastly, my son Jake, to whom this book is dedicated. Being an interior designer and a father are the two greatest joys in my life and definitely not in that order.

First published in the United States of America in 2018 by
Rizzoli International Publications Inc.
300 Park Avenue South
New York, NY 10010
www.rizzoliusa.com

Designed by Carrie Hunt, skylarkstudiosny.com

© 2018 Trip Haenisch

Distributed in the U.S. trade by Random House, New York.

Printed in China.

ISBN: 978-0-8478-6276-4
Library of Congress Control Number: 2018937413

2018 2019 2020 2021 / 10 9 8 7 6 5 4 3 2 1